ANGER MANAGEMENT WORKBOOK

Bajeerao Patil

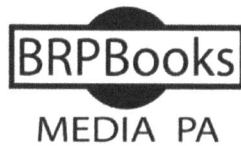

Copyright

Design & Layout by Prem Puthur
Printed in the United States of America
ISBN 978-0-9895698-4-2
Published by BRPBooks
307 Woodridge Lane
Media
PA 19063

This book is dedicated to my late cousin, Rajendra Patil, who was a victim of a suspended policeman's anger.

Author's Note

The names and other identifying characteristics of the persons included in this book have been changed to conceal their identities.

Acknowledgements

I owe a debt of gratitude to my father-in-law, Mr. Shankar Talekar, for his patience, valuable suggestions and constant encouragement. Additionally, I am thankful to my friend Prem Puthur for all his help and encouragement; without him I would not have been able to publish this book.

I am thankful to my children, Adwaita, Aditya and Arohi for being there for me when I needed to be entertained and be at ease.

I am thankful to my wife, Dipti, for helping me to realize my own anger and talking me into finding a solution to my own anger issues.

Finally, I am thankful to all my siblings, especially my brother, Jayant Patil, for being there for me through thick and thin.

Disclaimer

This book is written for people who have anger issues and are actively seeking help to manage their anger. The ideas, measures, and suggestions contained in this book are not proposed to replace the services of any trained professional. The author and publisher disclaim responsibility for any adverse effects resulting directly or indirectly from information contained in this book.

Contents

Section1

Anger and Emotions

Anger is one of the most **powerful emotions**. It is commonly experienced but often **handled very ineffectively.** We all experience anger from time to time, don't we? It only differs in degree: from mild annoyance, to frustration, to strong ferocity, to rage, and before you realize what's happening you lose complete control of your anger. Now instead of you handling your anger, your anger starts handling you. You lose sense of what's right and wrong and **you end up doing the wrong things**. When that happens you are only left with regret. Remember, if you add "D" before anger it becomes Danger.

The four stages of anger found in the learning module are:

Annoyance
Frustration
Infuriation
Hostility

Let me explain these stages to you through different experiences:

Annoyance: Annoyance is a state of mind wherein you are irritable or mildly angry, but only for a short period of time. It's like the wind – there one moment and gone the next. When I was in my early 20s, I had very low tolerance for loud music and people's insensitivity. *To some extent, I still have a lack of tolerance for many things including loud music and insensitivity, but with the passage of time I have mellowed down a great deal.* In the past, even the smallest things would easily annoy me. I would get annoyed when my mother would wake me up early in the mornings or when my dad would ask me to look after cattle or do some small chores around the house. I would think of saying something smart, but wouldn't say it because it would have been inappropriate or made my dad upset. Though the things were annoying, they weren't worth making a scene or losing my cool over. So, I would let it go and move on. The annoyance was always temporary and didn't force me to lose my temper. However, this is the stage where the anger begins to build. When you allow your annoyance to linger for long periods of time it turns into frustration. That's why annoyance is considered the build-up stage.

Frustration: We feel frustrated when we perceive that we are treated unfairly and cannot do anything about it. When I was in high school, my brother was looking for a government job but was unable to get one. He was completely frustrated with the corrupt system since he wasn't able to change it. He was of the opinion that the system was preventing him from making any progress. He was constantly expressing distress and annoyance. He would talk to anyone who would listen. His frustration wasn't helping the situation, it was only building up more anger in him. He was definitely angry, but wanted others to co-sign his anger. He was a tick away from boiling point. Fortunately, he did not act out or take out his frustration on others. I could see the spark of anger in him. This stage is also known as the spark stage.

Infuriation: In this stage you are extremely angry and impatient. You allow even insignificant things to infuriate you and you react impulsively. You lose control of your reactions and end up saying things that you don't mean to say. My friend Raj was indignant at being the object of social exploitation. His anger was provoked by his perception of the world around him. He thought the world was treating him unfairly. Sometimes, even the silence of other people infuriated him. He had trouble managing his anger. He reacted impulsively and always had an infuriating half-smile on his face.

Hostility: When you are hostile you are outright unfriendly and antagonistic. Your body language and gestures are aggressive. Others don't feel comfortable or safe in your company. You appear ready to fight or start trouble. Janet, a woman I know, is always hostile. She displays an attitude of intense ill will and acts like an enemy. She is unfriendly and antagonistic. However, she has trouble recognizing her hostility when confronted with it. She doesn't think there is anything wrong with being hostile. She reacts adversely and then regrets the aftermath, but still continues her hostile behavior.

What are the four stages of anger?

Remember: being annoyed, frustrated, infuriated, or hostile will not allow you to experience necessary peace of mind or live a healthy lifestyle. However, realizing the futility of being annoyed, frustrated, infuriated, or hostile will definitely help you get rid of your anger, and eventually you will be able to experience peace of mind. There are many important things in life, but **peace of mind tops the list**, doesn't it? For instance, if you had millions of dollars but no peace of mind, would you still enjoy those dollars? I don't think so! In the right state of mind, **you would definitely choose peace of mind over those millions of dollars**. Poorly managed anger can rob you of the peace of mind that you wouldn't trade for any amount of money or anything else. Remember, millions of dollars don't equal peace of mind.

Badly managed anger can also create problems for you at work, affect your relationships with others, and cause you stress and anxiety. Additionally, anger is capable of causing **biological** and **physiological** changes. When you are angry, your blood pressure and heart rate flares up. It also affects your energy hormones and adrenaline level negatively. **In a nutshell, anger can adversely affect the overall quality of your life.**

Anger is capable of creating an unsettling balance of mind, which not only hurts yourself but also hurts others around you. A moment of anger can send you to **jail, hospital** or even **kill you**. That's why you have to make a conscious decision to replace your anger with love or at least learn to manage your anger effectively. Anger impairs your judgment and forces you to act in a self-destructive manner. **When you are angry the negative energy flows within you**. You entertain negative thoughts and you begin scheming to get even with those who have wronged you or have hurt your feelings.

You might think getting angry is cool, that your anger is justified, that everyone gets angry, it's a natural emotion, you have every right to vent it the way you want and you can gain control over others or achieve much more quickly by getting angry than being patient. It's not fair to allow others to walk all over you. Wait – no one is expecting you to allow others to walk all over you or push you to the edge. Of course you are expected to stand for your rights, but in constructive ways. You have to be polite and assertive, and not aggressive. You will gain much more respect and feel good about yourself. And you will stay in control of your emotions and reactions.

Section 2

Exercises

Complete the following sentences:

Anger is one of the most--------------------------------It is commonly experienced but---

There are many important things in life, but------------------------------

Additionally, anger is capable of causing--------------and------------changes

A moment of anger can send you to----------,----------------or even------

Answer the following questions:

When you lose the sense of right and wrong what do you end up doing?

According to the author, if you are in the right state of mind, what would you do?

In a nutshell, what can anger do to you?

When you are angry, what kind of energy flows within you?

Some individuals are better equipped to handle their anger than others. Do you have trouble managing your anger? Yes! But the good news is you can also learn to manage your anger effectively provided you aren't in denial of your anger and want to gain control over your anger.

What is anger management?

Anger management is learning to recognize the basic source of your anger and feelings, and subsequently establishing the effective strategies to manage it.

Types of factors that cause anger

Internal and **external**

Internal factors are from within. They are directly connected to your body, mind and spirit. Here, we are referring to your ways of dealing with the stress in your life, your ways of reacting to the situations or events, your ways of handling your personal worries, your tendency to dwell in the past, your lack of patience, your inclination to hold resentments, and your unchecked expectations from others.

External factors are dynamic, or things that you do not have direct control over such as people, situations, government, problems at work, money problems, etc.

There is a notion that a certain amount of anger is necessary for survival. Anthony, a former patient of mine, had said that when he was in jail, his anger helped him to survive, and if it weren't for his angry outbursts he would have been a victim of physical, emotional and sexual abuse. Another school of thought maintains that anger motivates them to achieve their goals. But the question is, why use anger to achieve anything when you can achieve better things without being angry?

Even though anger is a natural emotion, expressing anger is a learned behavior that we use to defend ourselves when we feel threatened or attacked by others or our space is invaded.

Remember, different people express anger in different ways. Ultimately, how you express your anger makes the difference.

People express anger in the following ways:

Aggression: This is a very common way of expressing anger. **People who have trouble managing their anger resort to verbal or physical aggression. They become hostile and use profanity or threatening gestures or attack others physically.** In the United States alone, more than 31,000 die by guns each year – the figure includes suicides using guns. **One of the most influential factors in the development of aggressive behavior is upbringing.**

There are also others who express their anger by being passive aggressive. **They resort to putting people down or constantly criticizing or finding ways to hurt them indirectly.** Years ago, when I was working with a pharmaceutical company as a personnel and administration manager, I would frequently receive complaints about the lack of water supply in the toilet. We would get it fixed, but soon the problem would reoccur. We suspected that someone was doing it on purpose. So we decided to investigate the issue thoroughly. After grilling a couple of suspected employees, one of the maintenance employees confessed that he was twisting the pipe to cut the water supply in the toilet because he wanted to get the maintenance manager fired whom he hated.

Assertion: Being assertive doesn't mean being pushy or demanding. **It simply means you are confident and you possess the ability to get your ideas or feelings across to others without appearing intimidating or threatening.** At the same time, you don't allow others to walk all over you. Even in the face of difficulties you remain calm and act firmly without losing your composure or getting angry.

Suppression: Some individuals don't know how to express their anger appropriately, so they tend to suppress their anger until they can't keep it in any longer, and eventually they explode. A former patient, Wilson, had a tendency to suppress his anger. As much as he was forcibly trying to put an end to his angry feelings, he was feeling it more strongly inside and also had a ceaseless urge to express it. **Wilson's inability to express his anger appropriately caused him continuous inner turmoil, anxiety, stress and lots of frustration.** It was only after he learned that suppressing anger was unhealthy and there were better ways to channel his anger that things began to change for him. With sincere efforts, he learned to handle his anger appropriately. He began to think about the consequences of his angry outbursts, to walk away from the anger-producing situations, and to practice patience whenever he felt he was about to lose his cool. Finally, anger ceased to control him. Rather than trying to suppress your anger, your goal should be learning to express it appropriately.

Calming: It is not easy to calm yourself down when you are angry or agitated. Calming down requires **effort, patience and practice.** The patience helps in controlling outward behavior and also internal responses. Calming down includes taking steps toward reducing your heart rate and gaining control over your impulsive reactions. Just counting 1 to 10 or taking deep breaths repeatedly helps in anger producing situations. Of course calming down is difficult, but it is the most effective technique if done properly. Remember, **when you fail to calm down in an anger-inducing situation that's when your anger gets best of you.**

Answer the following questions:

According to the author, what do people do when they have trouble managing anger?

What is one of the most influential factors in the development of aggressive behavior?

What do passive aggressive people do?

What does being assertive mean?

What did Wilson's inability to express his anger appropriately do to him?

What does calming down require?

When does anger get the best of you?

Circle your answers: True or False

Anger is an emotion	True	False
Anger impairs judgment	True	False
Anger builds relationships	True	False
Suppressing anger is healthy	True	False
Anger cannot be controlled	True	False
Anger helps in maintaining health	True	False
Anger helps to reduce stress	True	False
Anger helps in gaining respect	True	False
Anger helps in decision making	True	False
Anger can cause stress	True	False
Anger can flare up blood pressure	True	False
Expressing anger is a learned behavior	True	False
Everyone is capable of managing anger	True	False
Angry outbursts can disturb peace of mind	True	False

	True	False
Thinking through the consequences when angry helps	True	False
Your reaction becomes an issue when it hurts you or others	True	False
No one has control over your reaction but you	True	False
Learning to manage anger takes work	True	False
Suppressing or ignoring anger is unhealthy	True	False
Venting anger inappropriately is unhealthy	True	False
Effective communication helps in managing anger	True	False
Angry people tend to jump to – and act on – conclusions	True	False

Total number
True	False
☐	☐

Does confronting people help?

Confronting people head-on isn't a problem when you do it for the right reason and in the right way, but **it becomes a problem when you do it for the wrong reason and in the wrong way.** When you decide to confront someone over any issue, you must gather all the facts before you confront that person, and you must know your reason for confronting the other person. Also, you must not be aggressive or sound confrontational while confronting others. Brian, another former patient, had a tendency of confronting people head-on. He confronted people just to satisfy his cunning ego. He was always aggressive and seemed to take lots of pride in confronting others. **He secretly craved to have the last word.**

When does confronting people head on-become a problem?

What did Brian secretly crave?

Initially, Brian had trouble accepting that he had anger issues and the way he confronted others was wrong. He maintained that he was just standing up for his rights. But one day, during an argument with one of his peers, he lost his cool and attempted to slap the peer. In defense, the peer punched Brian right in his face. Brian felt humiliated and cursed all his other peers, even though they had nothing to do with the situation. Later, Brian apologized for his behavior and accepted the fact that he had anger issues.

He took several psychological tests to measure the intensity of his angry feelings, what triggered his anger, and how well he handled his anger. The tests revealed the following:

1. He was quick to temper.
2. He wasn't able to control his angry feelings in anger-inducing situations, or manage his anger.
3. He had control issues and was intimidating.
4. He lacked proper communication skills.

5. He needed help to manage his anger.

When Brian began attending anger management classes his goal was to reduce the intensity of his emotions and the physiological arousal that caused him anger. In the past he used to think he could control people or get rid of them, but soon he learnt that it wasn't possible. He couldn't get rid of people or change them, but he could control his own reactions to any situation or event. Slowly but surely he was able to gain control over his anger, and communicate with others without being intimidating or threatening.

Let's take a test. Please circle your answers.

Are you comfortable in your own skin?   Yes or No

Do you think other people like your company?   Yes or No

Do you enjoy others' company?   Yes or No

Do you easily get irritable?   Yes or No

Do you suppress your feelings?   Yes or No

Do you have low tolerance for frustrations?   Yes or No

When things don't go your way do you act out?   Yes or No

Do you react aggressively during negative situations?   Yes or No

Do you expect things to go smoothly all the time?   Yes or No

Do you allow inconveniences to frustrate you?   Yes or No

Do people annoy you?   Yes or No

Do you talk ill of others?   Yes or No

Do you tend to curse, swear or speak in highly colorful terms? Yes or No

Do you think of teaching others a lesson?   Yes or No

Do you exaggerate situations and become over dramatic?   Yes or No

Do you blow things out of proportion?   Yes or No

Do you argue often?   Yes or No

Do you hold grudges against people?   Yes or No

Do you entertain negative thoughts?   Yes or No

Do you think of hurting others?   Yes or No

Do you feel justified in your angry outbursts?   Yes or No

Do you allow others to correct you when you are wrong?   Yes or No

Do you easily forgive others?   Yes or No

Do you think you have difficulty forgiving others?   Yes or No

Do you feel the need to argue with angry people to prove
your point?   Yes or No

Do you communicate with others appropriately?   Yes or No

Do you think you can control your reactions to any situation
  or event?   Yes or No

Total number
Yes or No

⬜ ⬜

Now let's work on another set of questions:

Do you think you have anger issues?   Yes or No

Do you consider the consequences of anger?   Yes or No

Do you think anger helps you?   Yes or No

Do you think anger helps anyone?   Yes or No

Do you think you can lose control when angry?   Yes or No

Do you think you can get in trouble because of your anger?   Yes or No

Do you regret your anger?   Yes or No

Do you have trouble expressing your emotions appropriately? Yes or No

Does anger give you a false sense of power or does
it make you feel "I won"?   Yes or No

                                                             Total number
                                                             Yes or No

                                                             ☐   ☐

Check the applicable answer

	Frequently	Sometimes	Rarely	Never
How often do you feel irritable or frustrated?	☐	☐	☐	☐
How often do you use curse words?	☐	☐	☐	☐
How often do you leave discussions?	☐	☐	☐	☐
How often do you think of taking revenge?	☐	☐	☐	☐
How often do you challenge others?	☐	☐	☐	☐
How often do you give others an angry look?	☐	☐	☐	☐
How often do you feel you are being challenged?	☐	☐	☐	☐

How often do you co-sign negativity? ☐ ☐ ☐ ☐

How often do you lose patience? ☐ ☐ ☐ ☐

How often do you complain about
unjust situations? ☐ ☐ ☐ ☐

How often do you hurt others? ☐ ☐ ☐ ☐

Total ☐ ☐ ☐ ☐

Make a list of things that trigger your anger:

What helps you to manage your anger?

Let's check your understanding of anger:

Patrick doesn't vent his anger aggressively, but he is always irritable and grumpy. Do you think he has anger issues?   Yes or No

Tracy doesn't always curse or throw things, but sometimes she withdraws socially and complains of being physically sick. She has a low tolerance for frustrations. Do you think she has anger issues?   Yes or No

James expects things to be smooth all the time. He can't stand inconveniences or annoyance. Do you think he has anger issues?   Yes or No

Katie doesn't like to be corrected even when she is wrong. Do you think she has anger issues?   Yes or No

Briana always talks negatively about others. Do you think she has anger issues?
                    Yes or No

Do you think taking things lightly and not complaining about unjust situations would help in reducing angry feelings?   Yes or No

Do you think keeping things simple would reduce angry feelings?   Yes or No

Do you think finding out the things that trigger anger and finding the strategies to keep those triggers from tipping over the edge would help in managing anger?
                    Yes or No

Do you think replacing negative thoughts with positive thoughts would help in managing anger?   Yes or No
                    Total
                    Yes or No

Suggestions:

Try relaxation techniques. Just lie in a chair and try to relax your muscles. When you're angry take deep breaths from your belly – it will definitely help you calm down.

Try positive self-talk: When angry, tell yourself, "I can handle this situation better, I need to take things easy, I don't need to lose my patience, I have to be nice and slow, I have to let the situation go, it's not worth wasting my time, I don't need to argue or fight, and I don't want to fight fire with fire." Finally, "I know how to handle things like grown-ups do."

Try to replace your thought process. Instead of telling yourself, "This is making me angry, I am going to get him, he is on my hot list, I want to teach him a lesson," say to yourself, "I'm upset, but I've got to let it go, teaching anyone a lesson wouldn't help the situation. It would complicate the situation further. I have better things to do. Wasting time on trivial things isn't worth it. I've got to move on, I'm done with this."

When you are in a heated argument the first thing to do is slow down. Tell yourself, "I have to slow down. I've to think before I say anything to avoid future trouble."

Try to remember effective handling of difficult situations in the past.

Try to count 1 to 10 repeatedly.

Try to meditate, or pray if you believe in prayers.

Try to remember humorous incidents in your life.

Take time out and think about the consequences of angry outbursts.

Work in the garden.

Go for a walk.

Listen to soothing music.

Spend time with your loved ones.

Make a conscious effort to use kind words.

Avoid all or nothing thinking.

Paint or draw if you like

Read self-help books

Share your feelings with someone you trust

You have to practice these techniques daily until you start using them automatically when you are faced against the odds.

Try to change your way of thinking. Remember, when you constantly entertain angry thoughts you turn into an angry person. Also remember that love combats anger.

Dos	Don'ts
Think about the consequences of anger	Don't justify your anger
Think before you act	Don't act without thinking
Make well informed decisions	Don't make hasty decisions

Control your anger	Don't allow anger to get the best of you
Control your impulsive behavior	Don't act on impulse
See the good things in the world	Don't be bitter with the world
Use proper language while communicating	Don't use curse words
Be friends with people with positive attitudes	Don't hang out with negative people
Be helpful	Don't think ill of others
Keep things simple	Don't complicate life
Encourage others to do right things	Don't instigate others
Be reasonable	Don't be demanding
Think positive	Don't dwell in negativity
Keep your expectations to a minimum	Avoid unreasonable expectations
Change your own attitude	Don't expect others to change
Watch comedy movies	Don't watch violent movies
Practice patience and tolerance	Don't be impatient

Control your emotions	Don't get carried away with emotions
Accept that you are just experiencing bumps in life	Don't make a mountain out of a molehill
Let go	Don't allow others to rent a space in your head

Do you demand fairness in life? Do you want others to appreciate you, and think that they should agree with you at all times? Do you demand that people should be more considerate and kind to you? We all want these things – that's natural – but angry people demand them, and when their demands aren't met they feel let down and become angry. 'Should' is a demand. You need to check your thinking. Reacting angrily is not normal. Feeling disappointed, frustrated or hurt comes naturally.

Answer the following questions:

Why do I tend to get angry?

How does it make me feel later?

Does my anger make me suffer? How?

Does my anger affect my relationship with others? How?

Do I feel the need to defend myself with angry people? If yes, why?

Am I able to make the right decisions when I'm angry?

Do you think you need help with your anger issues?

Section 3

Summary

Learning to manage anger takes work, but once you decide to do it and practice it daily you will definitely be able to manage your anger.

It is okay to feel angry when you have been wronged or put through unnecessary troubles. There is nothing wrong with the emotions – what matters is what you do with your emotions or how you react when faced against the odds. Your reaction becomes an issue when it hurts you or others around you. Remember, no one has control over your reaction but you.

When you are angry your judgment is clouded, and it doesn't allow you to think rationally or make well thought out decisions. Learning to express your anger appropriately can help you:

Feel good about yourself
Build better relationships with others
Make friends
Stay focused
Minimize stress in your life
Minimize anxiety
Minimize worries
Achieve your goals
Live a healthier lifestyle
Experience peace of mind

We all know that suppressing or ignoring anger is unhealthy, but venting it inappropriately is equally unhealthy. In fact, venting it inappropriately only adds fuel to the fire and reinforces your anger issues.

Some people maintain that when they are angry they get more power and others respect them more. This is untrue, but they believe their own impression and refuse to listen to other people's point of view. I don't think that people respect anyone who can't demonstrate appropriate control over their emotions. I think people respect and listen to those who show better control over their anger.

You will frequently come across people who always want to control the situations, for they don't know that isn't possible. At times, they are more focused on their feelings than controlling their reactions. Once they realize that they aren't in control of the situation, they resort to verbal and physical abuse. They are under the impression that when others push their buttons, they are left with no choice but to attack. However, when they understand that they don't have any control over situations and feelings but they do have control over their reactions and begin to practice assertiveness, things start changing for them and they learn to manage their anger effectively.

It will become easy for you to manage your anger effectively once you realize:
You cannot always be in charge of the situation that you are in
Feelings are natural, and are capable of making you feel uneasy at times
Only you can control only your reaction to any situation or event
You have no control over other people's behavior or attitude or reaction
You are capable of managing your anger effectively

Finally, if you still feel that you aren't able to manage your anger and it is really out of control, you should consider counseling to learn how to handle it better. Professionals can help you develop a range of personalized techniques to change your thinking and certain behaviors.